THIS uncover& discover BOOK

BELONGS TO

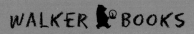

WALKER  BOOKS

WHO LIVES HERE?

Who lives in this warm, steamy jungle? Is it ...

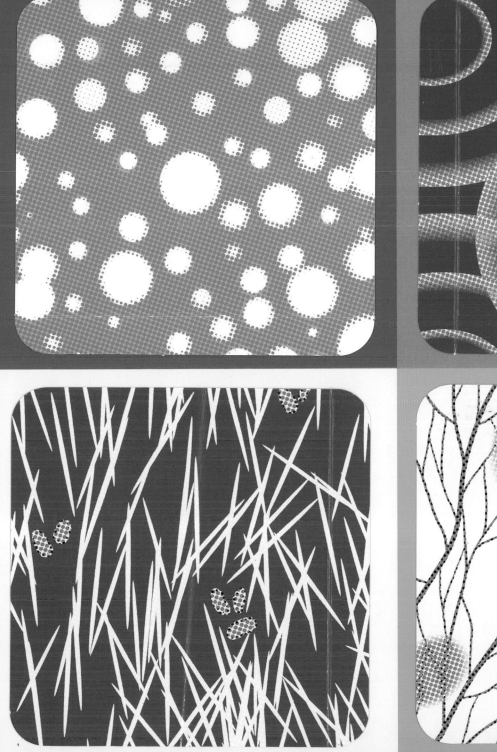
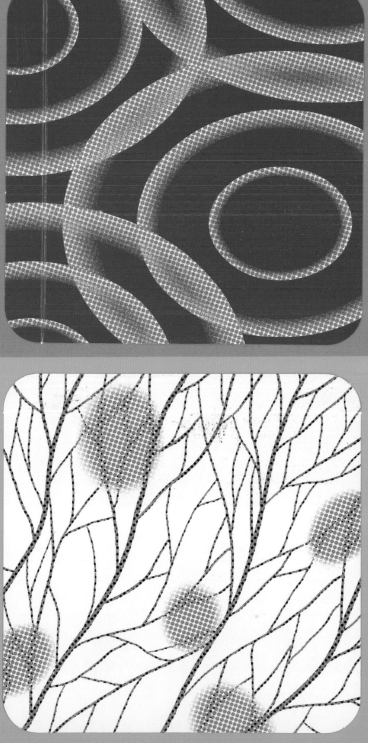

Sloth likes the warm, steamy jungle.
He hangs from branches by his long, strong
claws and eats leaves and snoozes all day.

LONG,
STRONG
CLAWS

WHO LIVES HERE?

Who lives in this still, cool pond?

Is it ...

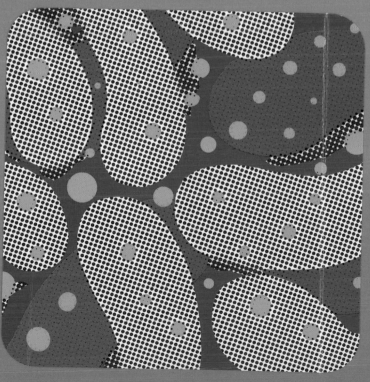

Dragonfly likes the still, cool pond.
She zooms around catching flies and lays
her eggs in the water.

EGGS

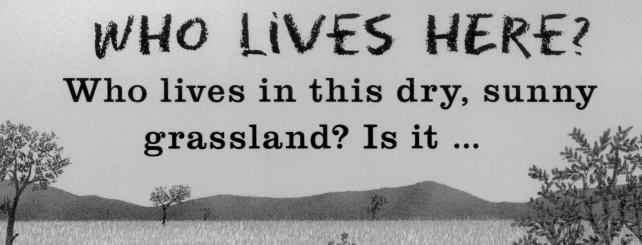

WHO LIVES HERE?

Who lives in this dry, sunny grassland? Is it ...

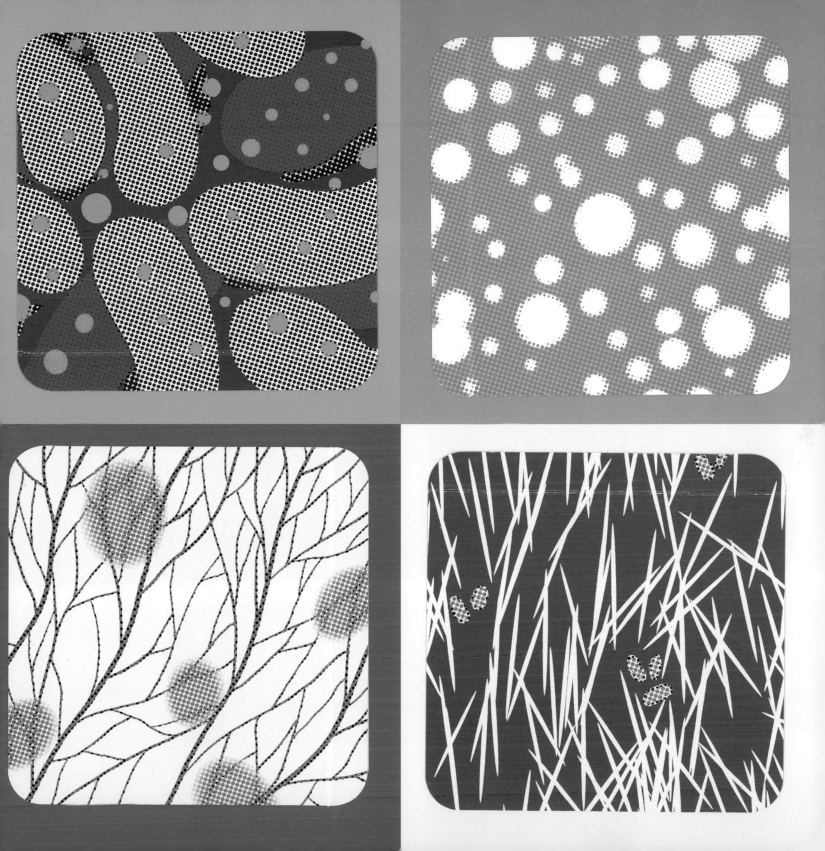

Meerkat likes the dry, sunny grassland.
He lives here with his big family.

DIGGING
FOR BEETLES

They watch out for
enemies and dig
in the sand
to find beetles
to eat.

WHO LIVES HERE?

Who lives on this coral reef in
the warm, clear, salty sea?
Is it ...

Clownfish likes the warm, clear, salty sea.
He lives hidden in an anemone where
he's safe and cosy.

ANEMONE

WHO LIVES HERE?

Who lives in the snowy, frozen Arctic near the icy North Pole? Is it ...

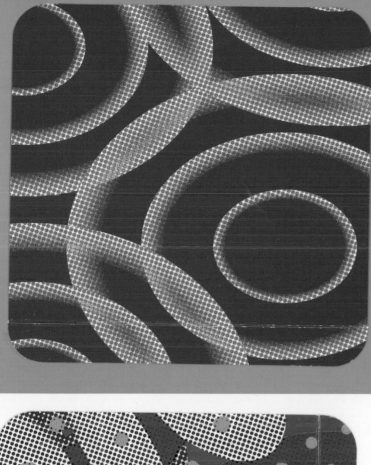
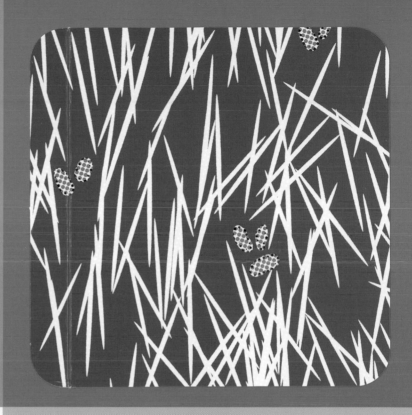
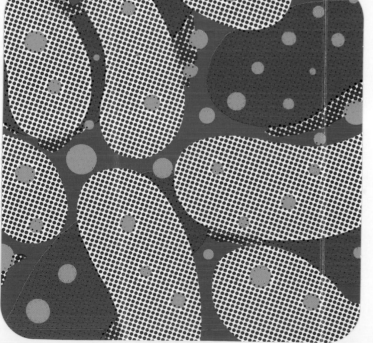

Polar bear likes the snowy Arctic.

THICK
FURRY COAT

She hunts for seals in the frozen sea.
Her thick furry coat keeps her warm
when it's colder than a freezer!

SEAL

Who lives with who?
Use the colours to
give you a clue!

jackal

banner fish

goldfish

gazelle

giant clam

toucan

polar bear

Arctic fox

pond skater

clownfish

sloth

snow goose

newt

meerkat

dragonfly

shark

howler monkey

cheetah

poison-arrow
frog

ringed seal

Who
lives
here?

First published 2012 by Walker Books Ltd
87 Vauxhall Walk, London SE11 5HJ

1 3 5 7 9 10 8 6 4 2

Text © 2012 Nicola Davies
Illustrations © 2012 Marc Boutavant

This book has been typeset in Print,
Clarendon T and Eraser

Printed in China

British Library Cataloguing in Publication Data:
a catalogue record for this book is available
from the British Library.

ISBN 978-1-4063-2811-0

www.walker.co.uk